CLASSICS Illustrated®

Edmond Rostand
CYRANO DE BERGERAC

essay by
Sherwood Smith, M.A.

ACCLAIM BOOKS
STUDY GUIDE

Cyrano De Bergerac

art by Alex Blum
adaptation by Ken Fitch
cover by Richard Case

For Classics Illustrated Study Guides
computer recoloring by VanHook Studios
editor: Madeleine Robins
assistant editor: Gregg Sanderson
design: Scott Friedlander

Classics Illustrated: Cyrano De Bergerac © Twin Circle Publishing Co.,
a division of Frawley Enterprises; licensed to First Classics, Inc.
All new material and compilation © 1997 by Acclaim Books, Inc.

Dale-Chall R.L.: 6.6

ISBN 1-57840-030-9

Classics Illustrated® is a registered trademark of the Frawley Corporation.

Acclaim Books, New York, NY
Printed in the United States

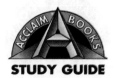

STUDY GUIDE

Cyrano de Bergerac

Illustrated by Alex A. Blum

By Edmond Rostand

ROXANE ROBIN

CHRISTIAN DE NEUVILLETTE

CYRANO DE BERGERAC

DE GUICHE

LE BRET

RAGUENEAU

This is the fantastic story of Cyrano de Bergerac, who lived in one of the most exciting and dangerous periods of the sensational history of France—about 1640. It is also the story of Cyrano de Bergerac's nose, a very large nose indeed. So sensitive was Cyrano about the size of his nose that he made himself his country's foremost swordsman defending it, became her most talked of poet in spite of it, and yet ran away from the one great love of his life because of it!

IF I HAD A RAPIER, I WOULD RUN YOU THROUGH!

OWWW!

STOP, CYRANO! STOP!

MY BOY! MY BOY! LET ME HELP YOU!

MAITRE, I WAS THINKING OF YOUR INTERESTS. BERGERAC WAS READING SWORDSMANSHIP BEHIND HIS LESSON BOOK!

PIG! SCUM OF THE GUTTERS! GET OUT OF THIS PLACE! NEVER RETURN! NEVER!

NEVER WILL BE MUCH TOO SOON, MONSIEUR!

THUS ENDED ABRUPTLY THE SCHOOLING OF CYRANO DE BERGERAC. WITH HIS FRIEND, LE BRET, HE WALKED SLOWLY AWAY FROM THE COLLEGE...

IT'S LIKE A WEIGHT LIFTED FROM ME, LE BRET! LIFE THERE WAS SO STALE IT WAS CHOKING ME!

YOU'RE TOO IMPULSIVE, CYRANO! YOU'LL NOT LIVE TILL YOU'RE TWENTY, THE WAY YOU CARRY ON. WHAT WILL YOU DO NOW?

PREPARE MYSELF FOR SURVIVAL, OF COURSE! DON'T FEAR FOR ME, LE BRET! I SHALL BECOME THE GREATEST SWORDSMAN IN ALL FRANCE!

THEN I'LL SAY AU REVOIR AND NOT GOOD-BYE. WE'LL MEET AGAIN-- I HOPE!

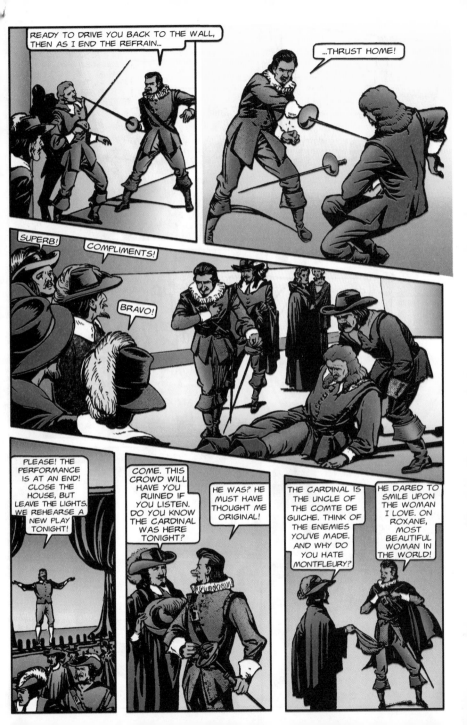

AT THE SIGNAL FROM THE LEADER OF THE MOB, THE SHADOWS AWOKE WITH MURDEROUS MOVEMENT!

GIVE ME YOUR LANTERN!

HA! RUSHING NEVER GOT ONE ANYWHERE!

IN FACT, I THINK IT WILL BE QUITE HOT FOR YOU, GENTLEMEN!

OW-W-W!

AIYYY!

AND THEN, AS I END THE REFRAIN...

As soon as the cadets left him, Christian turned to Le Bret...

CAPTAIN LE BRET, WHAT IS THE THING TO DO WHEN GASCONS GROW TOO BOASTFUL?

PROVE TO THEM THAT ONE MAY BE A NORMAN AND STILL HAVE COURAGE!

CYRANO, WE ALL CAME HERE TO LEARN ABOUT YOUR ADVENTURE LAST NIGHT!

YES, LET'S HEAR IT!

OH, VERY WELL!

NOW WHERE SHALL WE BEGIN? WELL, IT WAS SO DARK LAST NIGHT, YOU COULD NOT SEE BEYOND--

YOUR NOSE!

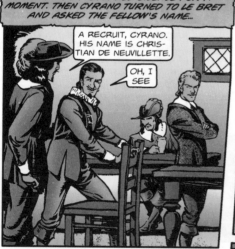

There was a stunned silence for a moment. Then Cyrano turned to Le Bret and asked the fellow's name...

A RECRUIT, CYRANO. HIS NAME IS CHRISTIAN DE NEUVILLETTE.

OH, I SEE

TO GO ON, SUDDENLY A SWORD FLASHED IN THE DARK. I CAUGHT IT FAIR--

ON THE NOSE!

WELL! A GREAT SUCCESS!

HELP ME CYRANO! I CANNOT LIVE UNLESS I WIN HER BACK--NOW! THIS MOMENT!

HELP YOU! IT'S MORE THAN YOU DESERVE! BUT WAIT! I'VE AN IDEA! DO YOU SEE THE LIGHT IN HER WINDOW?

STAND THERE. I'LL WHISPER TO YOU WHAT TO SAY. NOW CALL HER!

ROXANE!

WHO IS CALLING?

CHRISTIAN! I HAD TO TELL YOU...

NO, GO AWAY. YOU TELL ME NOTHING. YOU DO NOT LOVE ME ANY MORE!

NO--NO--NOT ANY MORE. I LOVE YOU EVERMORE-- AND EVER MORE AND MORE!

CYRANO SPOKE SO LOW THAT ROXANE COULD NOT HEAR...

HERE, THIS GROWS TOO DIFFICULT! LET ME DO THE TALKING! I'LL TAKE YOUR PLACE AND DISGUISE MY VOICE TO SOUND LIKE YOURS.

WHY, VERY GOOD! ONLY TELL ME, ARE YOU STILL THERE? WHY DO YOUR WORDS HESITATE?

MEANWHILE...ON A ROAD THROUGH NO MAN'S LAND...

THE SPANIARDS STOPPED THE COACH AND ASKED SEVERAL QUESTIONS. AT THE ANSWERS...

OH-H-H! THAT'S DIFFERENT! LET THEM PASS!

WITH THE SPANISH ATTACK IMMINENT, A RESTLESSNESS PREVAILED THROUGHOUT THE CAMP. AS THE HOURS PASSED, THE SOLDIERS CLUNG TO ANY MATTER THAT MIGHT LEAD TO EXCITEMENT...

IT HAS COME TO MY MIND THAT IF THE SUN SHINES BRIGHT FOR MANY DAYS MORE, IT WILL SHRIVEL YOUR NOSE DOWN TO PROPER SIZE. UNLESS, OF COURSE, YOU WEAR AN EXTRA HAT UPON IT FOR PROTECTION!

YOU'RE TIRED OF LIVING, I SEE! PREPARE!

I'LL LIVE TO BURY YOU WHERE YOU FALL! I'M READY!

WITH A SUDDEN TURN OF THE WRIST, CYRANO THREW BACK THE OTHER SOLDIER'S GUARD, AND THEN A THRUST AS FAST AS LIGHTNING ITSELF!

AS CYRANO'S OPPONENT FELL, A BOOK DROPPED FROM HIS JACKET...

HOT-HEAD THAT I AM! I'VE KILLED A LOVER OF POETRY! I MUST HONOR HIM! I MUST KILL ENOUGH OF THE ENEMY TO PAY FOR THOSE HE WOULD HAVE SLAIN!

BEFORE NIGHTFALL, ALL PREPARATIONS FOR WITHSTANDING AN ENEMY ATTACK HAD BEEN MADE. THEY NOW COULD ONLY WAIT IMPATIENTLY FOR WHATEVER MIGHT COME...

WHO GOES THERE?

ON THE SERVICE OF THE KING!

GOOD EVENING!

ROXANE!

BUT HOW DID YOU GET THROUGH THE SPANISH LINES?

I SIMPLY DROVE ALONG GOING WHERE THE MOUNTAINSIDE WAS LAID WASTE. WHEN THEY STOPPED ME I DROPPED MY EYES AND SAID, "I HAVE A LOVER."

YOU MUST LEAVE THIS PLACE AT ONCE. WE MUST TAKE YOU TO THE REAR. THIS POST IS DANGEROUS.

NO!

OH, I SEE! YOU'RE GOING TO FIGHT? I STAY HERE...WITH MY HUSBAND.

THEN, MADAME MAY WE HAVE YOUR HANDKERCHIEF FOR A BANNER? IT WILL MAKE THE FAIREST IN THE ARMY!

OF COURSE, YOU MAY HAVE IT.

IT MUST BE THIS FRESH AIR. I'M STARVING. RAGUENEAU, TIME FOR SUPPER.

YES, MADAME! GENTLEMEN, WILL YOU ASSIST ME?

HURRAH! WE'RE GOING TO EAT!

EAT? YOU MEAN WE'RE GOING TO FEAST!

CHEERS FOR MADAME DE NEUVILLETTE! CHEERS FOR RAGUENEAU!

THAT CAPTAIN THERE! A FINE SOLDIER WHO TRIES TO IGNORE ME! WELL, I'LL GET HIS ATTENTION BY TRICKERY!

WITH HIS CUSTOMARY QUICKNESS OF WIT, CYRANO CONCEIVED A WAY TO ATTRACT THE COWARDLY CAPTAIN...

AH...OH...I...I'M DYING!

SI, SEÑOR! I WEEL HELP YOU TO DIE, NO?

NO IS RIGHT, SEÑOR! YOU'LL NOT HELP ME TO DIE!

SO MUCH RANK AND SO MANY RIBBONS FOR SUCH A COWARD!

CYRANO! CYRANO!

THE SPANIARDS ARE IN FULL RETREAT! THE BATTLE IS OVER!

WHAT? OVER! AND I HAD JUST BEGUN TO FIGHT!

AND THAT HAND WITH WHICH YOU WRITE NEEDS HACKING OFF! I SHALL DO IT ON THE FIELD OF HONOR IF YOU'RE NOT AFRAID!

AFRAID? THAT'S A POINT OF HUMOR. COME, LET'S GO!

CYRANO SUMMONED HIS OLD FRIEND LE BRET TO ACT AS SECOND. WITHIN AN HOUR, HE WAS ON THE FIELD OF HONOR.

HA! YOU'RE HERE! LET THIS BE AN END OF IT.

I'LL MAKE A SUDDEN END OF IT FOR YOU, MONSIEUR!

HA! HA! IT'S TO BEGIN!

CA! CA! LET'S NOT WASTE ANY MORE TIME!

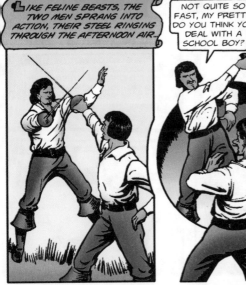

LIKE FELINE BEASTS, THE TWO MEN SPRANG INTO ACTION, THEIR STEEL RINGING THROUGH THE AFTERNOON AIR...

NOT QUITE SO FAST, MY PRETTY! DO YOU THINK YOU DEAL WITH A SCHOOL BOY?

A SCHOOL BOY WOULD NOT TRY SUCH STUPID STRATEGY AS YOU, MY LONG TONGUED FRIEND!

WITH THE SPEED OF A LIGHTNING FLASH, THE SWORDSMAN FIRST PARRIED AND THEN MOVED AWAY AND TO THE REAR OF CYRANO...

BUT CYRANO WAS NOT CAUGHT NAPPING. HE SWUNG ABOUT WITH THE MOTION OF HIS OPPONENT...

AND WITH A SWIFT, WELL-AIMED, WELL-TIMED BLOW...

AND THAT'S THAT! WHEN WILL THOSE FOOLS STOP HIRING ASSASSINS TO TRY TO KILL ME?

CYRANO'S CONSTANT BITTER ATTACKS UPON THOSE IN POWER MADE HIM MANY ENEMIES...

THAT INSOLENT WRETCH, DE GUICHE! THIS TIME HE HAS GONE TOO FAR, I SWEAR IT! HE'S SIGNED HIS OWN DEATH WARRANT!

AND WHO'LL DELIVER IT? HIS SWORD IS STILL POWERFUL, MY FRIEND!

TRUE! HE CANNOT BE CONQUERED BY THE SWORD. BUT THERE ARE OTHER WAYS TO DIE--WHO KNOWS? HE MAY HAVE AN ACCIDENT--SOON!

I KNOW. I HAVE EVERYTHING, HE NOTHING! YET I SHOULD BE PROUD NOW TO SHAKE HIS HAND...BUT HIS SATIRES HAVE MADE HIM MANY ENEMIES.

THEY STILL FEAR THAT SWORD OF HIS! IT'S NOT VIOLENCE I FEAR FOR HIM, BUT SOLITUDE-- POVERTY! IT SEEMS HE HAS WORN THE SAME OLD WORN SERGE SUIT FOR MANY MONTHS NOW...

IT'S TRUE ABOUT HIS SWORD. ONLY YESTERDAY HE DISPOSED OF A HIRED ASSASSIN. NEVERTHELESS, AT THE THEATER LAST NIGHT, I HEARD SOME THINGS. KEEP HIM HOME ALL YOU CAN. WHEN YOU SEE HIM TOMORROW, TELL HIM TO BE CAREFUL.

OH! I THANK YOU!

LATER, THAT SAME DAY...

THAT FINISHES THE SECOND ACT!

CYRANO, YOU'RE NOT LEAVING? WILL YOU NOT DINE HERE WITH ME?

MY REGRETS, RAGUENEAU. I HAVE A MAGNIFICENT ROAST WAITING FOR ME--A PRESENT FROM MY PUBLISHER!

POOR CYRANO! HE HAS NO ROAST WAITING! BUT HE'S SO PROUD!

AS CYRANO PREPARED TO LEAVE THE PASTRY SHOP, A MAN IN LACKEY'S CLOTHES, WHO HAD BEEN WATCHING HIM, SUDDENLY LEFT THE TABLE TO FOLLOW CYRANO OUTSIDE...

THE MAN PASSED OUTSIDE, BUT RAGUENEAU CALLED TO CYRANO, WHO STOPPED TO REPLY TO HIM...

AH, CYRANO, HAVE YOU SEEN MOLIERE'S NEW PLAY? HE STOLE A SCENE FROM YOU, WORD FOR WORD! IT PLAYED BEAUTIFULLY. THEY LAUGHED AND LAUGHED!

HE SHOWED GOOD TASTE IN STEALING MY PLAY...MOLIERE HAS GENIUS...CHRISTIAN HAD GOOD LOOKS. WITH ME 'TWAS ALWAYS THE SAME. GOOD NIGHT, MY FRIEND.

OUTSIDE THE PASTRY SHOP, THE MAN BECKONED...

WAIT HERE, ALMOST TO THE PASTRY SHOP, UNTIL I GIVE THE SIGNAL!

CYRANO EMERGED FROM THE SHOP AND WALKED DOWN THE STREET. THE MAN IN THE SHADOWS LET HIM GET SOME DISTANCE FROM THE SHOP, THEN FOLLOWED HALF WAY ACROSS THE STREET...

HO, THERE YOU! MONSIEUR OF THE LONG NOSE! LIAR! PLAGIARIST

INSOLENT LACKEY!

IF THE MAN WERE BUT ARMED, I WOULD CARVE HIM! BUT I'LL TEACH HIM A GOOD LESSON ANYWAY.

THE MAN STOPPED SUDDENLY IN THE ROAD AND MADE A SIGNAL...

THE CARRIAGE STARTED TO ROLL...

TOO LATE CYRANO BECAME AWARE OF HIS DANGER...

LATE IN THE AFTERNOON OF THE NEXT DAY...

SO LATE! HE SHOULD HAVE BEEN HERE AN HOUR AGO. HE WAS NEVER LATE BEFORE.

PERHAPS HE'S BEEN DETAINED.

AH! I HEAR HIM COMING NOW. I SHALL LEAVE YOU.

I'LL ATTEND TO MY EMBROIDERY AS IF I HAD NOT BEEN DISTURBED. OTHERWISE, HE MIGHT BE ANGRY WITH HIMSELF!

RACKED WITH PAIN, CYRANO REACHED THE CHAIR BESIDE ROXANE...

AFTER FOURTEEN YEARS...LATE FOR THE FIRST TIME!

YES. I WAS DETAINED BY A...A VISITOR. AN OLD ACQUAINTANCE WHO CAME MOST UNEXPECTEDLY.

I....I TOLD HIM TO RETURN IN AN HOUR...

PERHAPS A...A...LITTLE BEFORE DARK.

YOUR FRIEND WILL HAVE TO WAIT. I'LL NOT LET YOU LEAVE UNTIL DARK.

TELL ME ABOUT MY COURT NEWS, MY GAZETTE...

YES... THE NEWS. FRIDAY, THE 25TH: THE KING FELL ILL... AFTER EIGHT HELPINGS OF GRAPE MARMALADE. MARMALADE WILL... NO LONGER BE SERVED AT COURT. SATURDAY, THE 26TH...

SATURDAY... THE TWENTY-SIXTH... THE TWENTY-SI...

CYRANO! MY POOR FRIEND! WHAT IS IT?

NO, NO... IT IS NOTHING! MY OLD WOUNDS... IT WILL SOON BE GONE...

WE ALL HAVE OUR OLD WOUNDS. MINE IS HERE. IT IS HARD TO READ NOW... READ IT...

"FAREWELL, ROXANE, BECAUSE TODAY I DIE...

AS CYRANO READ, THE WORDS POURED BACK INTO HIS MEMORY...

...I KNOW THAT IT WILL BE TODAY, MY OWN DEARLY BELOVED--AND MY HEART, SO HEAVY WITH LOVE I HAVE NOT TOLD...

THAT VOICE! HOW I REMEMBER HEARING IT SO LONG AGO! STRANGE I HAD NOT NOTICED BEFORE! AND CYRANO'S EYES ARE CLOSED...YET HE REPEATS THE WORDS!

CYRANO DE BERGERAC
EDMOND ROSTAND

There are quite a few characters in literature and folk tales who are notable for the size of their noses: Pinnocchio is probably the most famous. There are real people famed primarily for their noble schnozzes—the actor Jimmy Durante comes to mind. In most of these cases, living or fictional, these folks are comic figures. In *Cyrano de Bergerac* the hero starts out as a comic figure, but by the end of the play we don't see him—or his nose—as funny anymore. His nose has become a symbol—as important to the audience as his soldier's crest is to Cyrano—of tragedy, of the outsider whose courage, loyalty, love, and honor make him someone lovable, not laughable.

The Author

Born 1868, Edmond Rostand—unlike Cyrano—actually was from the south of France. He went to Paris to complete his education, and there turned to writing plays.

Rostand's most popular
and enduring play is *Cyrano*, which was first acted in 1897, with the famous actor Constant Coquelin playing the lead. It was an immediate hit, and in short order the play was presented all over Europe and in the United States. Audiences seemed to welcome it as a relief from the current fashion for grim realistic plays from the Naturalists and Symbolists.

He wrote other plays, of course, but the only play of his that is still remembered is *L'Aiglon*, which was first produced in 1900. It is a patriotic tragedy in six acts, based on a real historical person, the Duke of Reichstadt; this play was written to display the talents of the world-famous actress Sarah Bernhardt.

He was elected to the Academie Francaise in 1901, and created an officer of the French Legion of Honor, while he was in his early thirties—the highest honors for a French writer. He was unfortunately a sickly man his entire life, and in later years he was so ill he withdrew to the south to recover and work on his writing. It took ten years to produce his last play, which was not a success. He died just three weeks after World War I ended.

When Edmond Rostand's play *Cyrano de Bergerac* was first produced in 1897, after years of grim ultra-realistic plays, its romance, its wit and dash and pathos dazzled audiences. By the third act, there probably wasn't a lady in the audience who didn't wish that someone like Cyrano would court her—big nose notwithstanding—and likewise the men watching might have wished, even for a short time, that they could live such an adventurous, romantic life. Philosopher, wit, noble and courageous, Cyrano's ultimately tragic life is the kind that uplifts the spirits. It's no wonder the play is still being acted the world around, and movies based on it have been made as recently as five years ago.

Plot

The play is written in five acts, and the original French form is in alexandrine rhyming couplets. This form is much like the classical drama of Cyrano's period.

Act One opens at the Hotel Bourgogne. Many in the audience wonder if the actor Montfleury will play—or if Cyrano will show up, having

The Alexandrine Form

The Alexandrine line is made up of twelve syllables combined into six two-syllable "feet" (called iambic hexameter). Hexameter means six feet; iambic means that the second syllable in each foot is accented. So an alexandrine line might read something like this:

I said when I recalled my younger days abroad

amid the golden spires that ringed the village round...

Cyrano de Bergerac is written in alexandrine couplets, which means the lines were organized in rhyming pairs. So our couplet might read:

I said when I recalled my younger days abroad

amid the golden spires, and heard the bellsong's laud...

issued a threat. Christian, newly arrived from the north of France, finds Ligniere, a writer, and begs for information about Roxane, whom he has fallen in love with from afar. He's worried that she might be clever, one of the *precieuses* and thus would look down on a plain, simple soldier. Ligniere assures him that she is indeed well-read—but that the haughty, powerful Comte de Guiche is also in love with her, and is trying to force her to marry one of his toadies, Vicomte de Valvert, so that he can court her without recrimination. She is also cousin to the infamous Cyrano—and Ligniere describes a dashing, highly courageous man.

Christian does not see Cyrano; instead, he discovers a plot to have Ligniere assassinated, and goes off to warn the poet. Meanwhile, the performance is about to start—and Cyrano is heard from the balcony. Amid excitement from the watching audience, he routs Montfluery and sends him scuttling off. When the theatre owner pleads for reimbursement for the ruined performance, Cyrano grandly throws him a bag of coins. "You can close the theatre any time you want!"

Everyone except de Guiche—who likes Montfleury—and his followers are impressed. A busybody demands to know who Cyrano's patron is, and is grandly told that the poet refuses to have a patron. His freedom and honor are too important. Cyrano then demands, "Are you looking at my nose?" The busybody scampers off, saying that Cyrano's nose is very small.

Valvert, de Guiche's toady, swaggers up and says, "Your nose is large!" "Is that the best you can do?" Cyrano retorts, and he embarks on a long, funny catalogue, divided into categories such as "Aggressive," "Friendly," "Thoughtful," "Pedantic" and "Practical"—of all the insults that an imaginative man might have made: "I sir, if that nose were mine, I'd have it amputated!"

The list of insults infuriates Valvert,

UNLESS THOSE GENTLEMEN RETAIN THEIR SEATS, MY SWORD MAY BITE THEIR RIBBONS! WELL, MONTFLEURY, STILL NO EXIT?... VERY GOOD. THEN I ENTER WITH KNIFE--TO CARVE THIS FAT STUFFED GOOSE!

Ragueneau's shop the next day. Delighted, Cyrano goes off and routs single-handed the hundred men who were lying in wait for Ligniere.

who hurls the worst insult he can come up with at Cyrano: "Poet!" Cyrano not only agrees, he proposes to put together a poem as he fights Valvert—and true to his word, on the last line, he thrusts "as I end the refrain!"

Afterward Cyrano admits to Le Bret that he has no money now—that bag was all he possessed. Le Bret admonishes him, but Cyrano shrugs; what is starvation when one can make such a magnificent gesture? He then admits that he is in love, and on being pressed, tells Le Bret that the lady is his cousin, Roxane. Le Bret urges him to speak, but Cyrano won't. What woman could love that nose? But directly after, Roxane comes up and whispers that she must talk to Cyrano about something very important, and they arrange to meet at

Act Two takes place at the Pastry Shop. Cyrano is writing a love letter as Ragueneau—a poet himself—happily gives away pastries to his favorite hungry poets. He is not a good business man—he loves poetry more than profits—and his wife Lise nags him about it.

Roxane appears, and talks fondly of the good times she and Cyrano had as children, and how she always looked up to him. She tells him she is in love, and describes a noble character. But just as it seems he is about to admit to his love, she says that her beloved is handsome.

Cyrano knows at once that she does not mean him; and Roxane names Christian, adding that he has recently joined Cyrano's company of guards. She begs Cyrano to watch out for Christian, which he promises to do.

She leaves, and the cadets of Castel-Jaloux' company arrive, all wanting to hear the story of Cyrano's exploits against the hundred men the night before. The Comte de Guiche also arrives, and tries to win Cyrano over with promises of a great patron. But Cyrano is instantly on his guard; he sees in the offer an attempt to muzzle him, and he refuses. De Guiche is not pleased, especially when the story comes out—and it appears that de Guiche was the one who hired the hundred men. He promises there will be trouble for Cyrano and his company of "Mad Gascons" alike—which, of course, cheers the blood-thirsty cadets enormously.

Then Cyrano starts telling his story, but he is constantly inter-rupted by a handsome young man who keeps making refer-ences to his nose. The cadets all wait breathlessly for Cyrano to annihilate this newcomer, but Cyrano, on learning that this is the new recruit, Baron Christian de Neuvillette, keeps his tem-per...for a time. Then, suddenly, he throws everyone out of the room. The cadets all go outside, waiting expectantly to hear the sounds of the Baron being munched. Instead, Cyrano embraces the surprised Baron, compliments him on his courage, then says that Roxane has mentioned him. Christian is happy—until he admits that he doesn't know how to court an elegant, well-read woman. He's just a simple, plain-spoken sol-dier. Cyrano pulls out his letter, says it's just something he dashed off, and embarks Christian on his courtship. When they go out together, the cadets are amazed—but when one makes a remark about noses, Cyrano knocks him down, and the cadets are glad that he's his old self again.

Act Three. The three-way courtship flourishes. Roxane is delighted by the wonderful let-ters she receives, and at first Christian is thrilled. Cyrano watches from afar, in turns anguished because he cannot express his love directly, and delighted that his coaching and letters have such an effect. Roxane makes it clear that she is falling in love with the man whose poesy is so thrilling—yet she insists she could not love a plain man any more than she could a stupid one.

De Guiche comes, saying that the guards are all being ordered

THEY GROPE IN THE DARKNESS TOWARD THE LIGHT OF YOU! YOUR NAME IS LIKE A GOLDEN BELL HUNG IN MY HEART. AND WHEN I THINK OF YOU, I TREMBLE, AND THE BELL SWINGS AND RINGS-- ROXANE! ROXANE!

YES, THAT IS LOVE! YOU NEVER SPOKE TO ME LIKE THIS! EVEN YOUR VOICE SOUNDS DIFFERENT!

TONIGHT I SPEAK FROM MY HEART FOR THE FIRST TIME! IT'S MY VOICE MINE, MY OWN, THAT MAKES YOU TREMBLE THERE IN THE GREEN GLOOM ABOVE ME!

YES, I DO TREMBLE-- AND I WEEP--AND I LOVE YOU--AND I AM YOURS--AND YOU HAVE MADE ME YOURS!

to Arras to besiege the Spanish. Roxane, fearful of danger to Christian, gets a clever idea: she exhorts de Guiche to leave Cyrano's company in Paris. "Put Cyrano in the front lines, which he adores? If you want to make him mad, leave him behind!" De Guiche is happy to do so.

Christian decides he wants to court Roxane on his own—to be himself. He meets Roxane when she is returning from Madame Clomire's salon, and proclaims his love. She asks him to embroider on the theme, and he repeats that he loves her. Roxane is annoyed; she thinks his courting stupid. Where are his pretty words?—it's as bad as if he were no longer handsome. Roxane at this point is very like the *precieuses* (see below): superficial, interested more in the pretty words and the way they are said than in their con-

tent or sincerity. She flounces away, and Christian is in despair. Cyrano comes to his rescue. They call to her below her balcony. She comes out, but is impatient until Cyrano supplies the words for Christian to court her with high-flown poesy. It is slow and awkward, so, safe in the darkness, for the first time Cyrano speaks directly, talking of love so intoxicatingly that Roxane permits Christian to climb up and kiss her.

They are then interrupted when a friar appears with a letter from de Guiche, saying that he will come to see her once more before the companies march to war at dawn. Roxane does not let anyone see it, but insists to the friar that he was sent by the Commander in order to marry her to Christian. Cyrano she begs to keep de Guiche away for fifteen minutes, until the ceremony is safely performed.

Cyrano covers his nose with his cloak and drops down in front of de Guiche, talking like a madman. He claims he's just arrived

from a visit to the moon, and despite his annoyance at being stopped, de Guiche is interested. But when the time is up, Cyrano reveals himself—and also the plot. Furious, de Guiche changes the orders, and informs Cyrano and Christian that they will be marching with the others at dawn.

Act Four. The siege has been dragging on, and the Spanish have trapped the French, which means they are surrounded by enemies and have no supplies. Cyrano returns from his daily trip through enemy lines to deliver his letters to Roxane. The men complain of hunger, and Cyrano exhorts them to tighten their belts and think of Gascony. When de Guiche arrives, the men pull out their cards and pipes, acting as if they were on a picnic. De Guiche tries to impress them, describing an action he

was in the day before, in which he had to throw away his sash of command so that he could get through safely as a "common soldier." Cyrano says that a truly heroic commander would never throw down his sash and relinquish the honor of being fired at—and when de Guiche challenges him, Cyrano produces the sash, which he picked up on one of his expeditions.

Angrily, de Guiche uses it to give a signal to a Spanish spy—this is the place that the Spanish should launch their next attack. In revenge for their lack of respect for de Guiche, the Mad Gascons will have the honor of being at the very front of the fighting. Cyrano gives Christian a last letter, in case he is killed. Christian's suspicions are roused, but there's no time for discussion for a surprise occurs—Roxane arrives with

Ragueneau in tow. De Guiche and Cyrano both try to get her to leave, and are embarrassed to admit the peril the cadets are in (and the reason for it). When Roxane figures it out, she maintains she will stay—she has the right to die with her husband. De Guiche leaves.

Roxane then reveals that her carriage is full of food, and the Gascons have a grand meal; in the meantime, Cyrano corners Christian and admits that "Christian" has been writing Roxane every day, sometimes twice! De Guiche reappears, having found a cannon for the defense, and at first the cadets hide the feast. The Commander

her despite deadly danger—have caused her to regret her shallowness, and she begs his forgiveness for having loved him for his beauty alone. Christian is more and more dismayed, especially when she says that she would love him even if he were ugly. Christian goes to Cyrano and insists that it is he who Roxane truly loves—and he knows now that Cyrano loves her equally. An honest and courageous man even though he is no poet, Christian was content enough to let Cyrano do his courting if that was what pleased his lady, but now that he's discovered that they love one another, he will no longer stand in the middle to take advantage of either of them. He tells Cyrano to confess everything to Roxane. Cyrano begins. Roxane assures him that her love has matured, and

WITH TWO OF THE THREE ADVERSARIES DOWN, CYRANO TURNED ON THE THIRD ENEMY WITH THE SWIFTNESS OF A TIGER AT THE MOMENT OF THE KILL!

THREE IN SUCCESSION AND WITHOUT A SCRATCH TO MYSELF! THE SPANIARDS WILL NOT SOON FORGET THIS BATTLE!

tries to get Roxane to leave, but when she refuses he says he will stay and die with them. The cadets welcome him as one of their own, and the feast reappears. Roxane then comes to Christian and says that the letters she received—delivered to

now she would love Christian for his soul alone, even if he were ugly—but before Cyrano can confess, the Spanish attack. Christian makes a charge and is mortally wounded. Cyrano whispers to him that he told Roxane but it was Christian she truly loved, and Christian dies. Ragueneau and the others spirit the grieving Roxane away, and the cadets go into heroic battle, Cyrano in their midst. (See previous page)

Act Five, fifteen years later— 1655. De Guiche arrives at the convent where Roxane has been living since the Siege of Arras, mourning her lost love. She keeps Christian's last letter with her always. De Guiche admits that though he has accrued even more honors, and poor Cyrano has just gotten poorer, making enemies all around for his savage attacks against hypocrisy, fools, and cowards, he would be honored to shake his hand. He tells Roxane to warn Cyrano that he overheard a plot to kill him. She promises to warn him when he arrives at sundown, which he has done faithfully every Friday.

But Cyrano is late, and he moves slowly in the gathering darkness. He begins to give Roxane his personal "Gazette"—gossip about the royal court—but halfway through stops and gasps. He then asks if she still has Christian's last letter, and reminds her that she once promised he could read it. But when he begins, unnoticed dark has fallen, yet he still reads on. Roxane suddenly recognizes the voice from under the balcony, and sees that he knows the letter—and then Cyrano falls over, and reveals that he was attacked by a falling log (in the Classics Illustrated adaptation he is struck down by a speeding coach). Roxane is devastated; she has all along loved only one man, but she has lost him twice.

Cyrano's friends rally to his side, but he won't face death sitting down. He swings his sword at the ghosts of all the ills he spent his life fighting, and at the last he dies, saying that one thing has been left to him: his "panache".

All three of the main characters by the end have attained heroic stature. Christian, when he realizes the truth and is willing to sacrifice his love for the two who love one another—and then goes off to fight and be killed. Roxane, who realizes that she has been shallow and superficial, and rides gallantly to her beloved's side. And Cyrano who was denied the hero's death he desired. Denied love, denied fame for his poetry (just before he dies, Le Bret tells him that Moliere has stolen a scene from one of his plays), he has only his honor, which he never once compromised.

Panache

The word 'panache' carries a double meaning, and if you look at different translations of the play, some will end with 'panache' while others will say 'stainless white soldier's plume' or something like it. The initial meaning of the word is the plume of feathers on a war helmet. It came into use just before Rostand employed it so memorably in his play—but this word, which ends Cyrano's story, has come to mean honor, style, and courage.

CYRANO... ONE THING IS MINE OWN! WITHOUT STAIN, UNSPOTTED FROM THE WORLD!.. MY *WHITE PLUME!*

Characters

Cyrano was Real?

Actually, most of the speaking parts in this play are based on real people, though Rostand took some liberties with the truth—sometimes on purpose, and sometimes not. By the time he wrote this play in the 1890s, there were a number of legends about the real Cyrano—some that we now know are false—that he drew on.

So Cyrano de Bergerac was in fact a real person, and though the one drawing extant depicts a long nose, there is no evidence that it was the cause of his boisterous life.

Savinien Cyrano de Bergerac was born in 1619 in a small town just outside of Paris. Thus, he was not a Gascon but a Parisian. His early years were spent at the College Beauvais, where he was quarrelsome and unruly—as the beginning of the Classics Illustrated adaptation shows. (See following page.)

As a young man he joined a company of guards, and was wounded at the siege of Arras in 1640. He subsequently gave up the military and turned to philosophy and writing. Though his friend Le Bret later wrote that he was sober and chaste, there is evidence that he was involved with various love affairs—mostly with men in his circle of philosophers and poets. (The most famed was with Dassoucy, who

is mentioned in the play.) He did have a cousin, **Madeleine Robin (called Roxane)**, but there is no evidence that he was in love with her. There is also no evidence that he fought duels over his nose. He studied under Pierre Gassendi, a Paris mathematician and philosopher who was not at all liked by the authorities.

Cyrano wrote his two best-known works, *Histoire comique des etats et empires de la lune* (*Comic History of the States and Empires of the Moon*) and *Histoire comique des etats et empires du solei* (*Comic History of the States and Empires of the Sun*), around 1654, and they were published after he died. These books are among the first examples of sci-

ence fiction ever written. They make fun of political and religious figures of Cyrano's times, and mix in many scientific theories. Cyrano helped to popularize scientific theory—one of the concepts he predicted was the atomic structure of matter—but he especially loved poking fun at authorities and encouraging freethinking materialism.

He also wrote plays. His *La Mort d'Agrippine* got him into trouble for blasphemy (over a single misinterpreted line), but it contains ideas that were daring for his time, and the tragic dialogue made it interesting drama. His comedy *Le Pedant Joue* was full of foolery and fun, which went against the classical tastes of the time, but it was read by his contemporaries—as the play mentions, Moliere really did borrow a couple of its scenes for his famous play *Les Fourberies de Scapin*.

Cyrano also did some political writing. His most famous piece was a scathing denouncement of the Frondeurs—aristocratic rebels who tried, more than once, to wrest control of the government from the Queen and Cardinal Mazarin. The Frondeurs' chief political goal was to hold on to powers which Mazarin was trying to win from them in his attempts to reform the government. Cyrano probably supported the intended reforms, and defended Cardinal Mazarin for his political realism. This didn't prevent him from denouncing the cardinal violently for other policies he *didn't* approve of!

Cyrano was at all times a radical and freethinker. He was indeed hit on the head by a falling piece of wood, and such was his reputation there were many who whispered of plots and conspiracies against him. He died in 1655.

Montfleury was a real actor—a favorite of Cardinal Richelieu, who was a patron of the arts. Montfleury mostly played kingly roles, he was apparently rather fat, and there is evidence that the real Cyrano loathed him, though there is no record of the challenge of Act I.

The **Comte de Guiche** was also a real man. Married to Cardinal Richelieu's niece, he was very influential at court. In Madame de Sevigny's letters, where he is mentioned frequently, he appears to be an honest, hard working, courageous man, who devoted his entire life to his country. He was very popular, and when he died, he was sincerely grieved.

Roxane did indeed marry a **Baron de Neuvillette**, but his name was not Christian. When he died at the siege of Arras, she did retire to a convent.

Ragueneau did apparently have a pastry shop, and the various members of the Hotel Bourgogne theatre (which was a real theatre attached to a wing of the palace of the Dukes of Burgundy) were real.

Salonistes and Precieuses

The key to this play is Roxane's initial shallow and superficial insistence on being beautifully courted by a beautiful man. She is quite clearly a *precieuse* ("precious one," meaning a fussy, overly refined person), for we see her going off to the salon of Madame Clomire. This salon would be copying the fashion set by the great salonistes: the Marquise de Rambouillet, and Mademoiselle de Scudery.

The Rambouillet salon was the first. This remarkable woman, who made a happy and lifelong marriage at the age of twelve, was already educated and fluent in three language when she married. When she was brought to Paris, she disliked the dirty, uncouth barracks-room atmosphere of the Royal Court of Henri IV (father of Louis XIII) and so she set up her own society, first redesigning the Hotel (the word meant a kind of mansion or palace in the city) de Rambouillet. In these congenial, artistic, and clean surroundings, she brought together the best educated people in noble society, and her salons influenced intellectual life in Paris for fifty years. Literary reputations were made and lost in her salons. Famed playwrights read their plays there; philosophers discussed their ideas; even the well-known priest, Father Bossuet, is said to have preached his first sermon at her salon. The Hotel was lost in the troubles of 1649, and the Marquise was getting old and sickly, but her style—in hotels, and in salons—had been set for good and ill.

There was always the danger that a focus on refinement would become an end in itself, and with lesser minds this certainly happened. A second salon in the latter half of the century was ruled over by Mlle. de Scudery. She was a woman who made her living writing novels; for a time everyone in France read them, and there are references to her characters in the letters and diaries of all the great people of the time. Her "Saturdays" drew not just literary figures, but persons who wanted to be known for their great refinement—most notably, her lifelong admirer, a man named Paul Pellison. To him, the turn of a phrase was more important than its content; he decreed that "a thought is worthless if it can be understood by the vulgar." It was this influence that caused such sillinesses (in the name of refinement) as "Useless one, remove the superfluity of this ardency" for "Servant! Put out the candle." And instead of saying, "It's raining," one must make a scientific or Classical allusion, such as, "The third Element is descending." Moliere, quite rightly, lampooned this kind of pompous behavior in his farcical play, *Les Precieuses Ridicules*

The implication in Rostand's play is that Madame Clomire's salon was probably one of the many copies of the Scudery model—and its superficial influence was something that Roxane overcame too late for her to recognize the truth about Cyrano—and Christian.

The play spans fifteen years, starting at the end of the reign of Louis XIII, and ending at the beginning of the reign of Louis XIV, also known as the Sun King.

Louis XIII was a weak king, much overshadowed by the powerful, complex figure of Cardinal Richelieu, his prime minister of state, who devoted his life to consolidating royal power in France, and achieving France's natural borders. Richelieu also conducted two protracted wars, against the Spanish outside the borders, and against the Huguenots (French Protestants) within it.

Louis XIV was born late in his father's life. When Louis XIII and Richelieu died, one right after the other, the future Sun King was a small boy. His mother, the bright, lovely Queen Anne, and Cardinal Mazarin took over the regency, and together they sought to maintain royal French power for the boy. (There is a brief mention in Cyrano's Gazette of the "Mancini almost becoming a queen"; Louis XIV, while still a very young man, fell desperately in love with the beautiful and good Marie Mancini, Mazarin's niece, and almost married her. It took all the power his mother, the Cardinal, and others had over the young king to force him to give up his love and marry as kings must—his cousin, the Infanta of Spain—to assure a treaty. It didn't help that the poor Infanta was mentally a child, and was small and odd-looking.)

There are several brief mentions of army life through the play. At one point during Act Four, when de Guiche is angry with the Gascons and demands to know whether he should have them punished, their captain retorts that he can't punish them—only the captain can, for it is he who pays them—and his orders come straight from the high command.

The organization of the army in these years was notoriously corrupt. Captains did indeed hire and pay (more often they cheated) their men. At the top of the command there were more often than not very young noblemen who had never seen battle; during the time of the early part of the play, most of the war in the Netherlands was commanded by the very young Duke of Enghien, a cousin to the king, who fortunately turned out to be a brilliant commander. (See following page.) But war was rough, discipline lax, and most of the time equipment and supplies were foraged from the neighboring civilians in the countryside (no matter whose side they were on)—at sword's point. It was later, under Louis XIV, that the King's war minister, the Marquis de Louvois, undertook to reform the army, and drastic changes were made—but those took place after Cyrano's death.

Marriage customs, particularly among the aristocrats, were different from now. One married for life, but not necessarily for love. Usually one married (as kings had to) in order to gain prestige or fortune for one's family. Thus we have the Comte de Guiche, married to the niece of the powerful Cardinal Richelieu, trying to maneuver Roxane into marriage with one of his followers so that he can court her. (Then, as in most of history, it was much easier for men to play around than for women—especially unmarried women.)

During the 17th Century, French literature flowered. Brilliant writers were born during this time, and flourished due

FIGHTING FIERCELY, CYRANO SPRANG FROM THE WALL TO THE GROUND AS SPANIARDS SWARMED LIKE FLIES UPON THE FRENCH...

DROP YOUR MUSKETS, CADETS! THIS IS GOING TO BE HAND-TO-HAND FIGHTING!

Gazettes

A kind of newspaper that ostensibly reported on court news, but was really more of a gossip column. It reported daily events in the life of the royal court, always praising those in power, and gave other news only as the authorities saw fit to release it. There were, of course, many street 'gazettes' that were not at all under the control of the authorities. They criticized government, ministers, and many years later, the royal family itself. These were enormously popular, and hard to stamp out. Of course, when Roxane speaks of Cyrano as her 'gazette,' she means that he brings her all the news—and his amusing opinions of it, too.

to attention from royalty and nobility: Cardinal Richelieu, himself fond of plays and poetry, gave official recognition to a group that would later form the *Acadamie Francaise.* Corneille, Descartes, Moliere were just a few of the names of writers of the period. Many were encouraged in the salons of the intellectuals (mostly women) and thus established careers. Aristocrats valued education, and many tried their hands at writing plays and poetry, or got together to read histories and philosophers.

ty—to the people he loves, and to his ideals. It is the latter which eventually kills him, for not all the world values someone who remains steadfastly

ANOTHER SATIRE FOR THE GAZETTE? CYRANO, WHY DO YOU DO IT? WHY DO YOU ATTACK...

STUPIDITY, DECEIT, CORRUPTION? BECAUSE I'M TOO OLD TO CHANGE!

honest, pointing out "Falsehood! Compromise! Bigotry! Cowardice! Folly!" in the great as well as the unimportant people. Loyalty is an important part of the play for all the characters: poor Ragnueneau, whose nagging wife finally runs off with a Musketeer; Le Bret, who stays friend to Cyrano even when his unpopularity grows to dangerous proportions; de Guiche, who despite his achievements, is delighted to be accepted by the Mad Gascons (proving, at the point of death, his real loyalty—which he acts on again by warning Roxane of impending danger to his former enemy, Cyrano); Christian, who submits to someone else conducting his courtship out of loyalty to his lady—and then chooses death in order to free her and the man she truly loves.

Themes

"All that glitters is not gold" is a very common theme in literature, and has been for centuries. Cyrano, the great and noble poet who is marred by his ugly nose, is not valued by the woman he loves until it is too late. Christian, whose handsome face first attracts Roxane, does not possess the poetic soul that she also craves. Roxane does not know how to value either of them; she does not want, at first, just to be courted by a handsome man, she wants to be courted beautifully.

But the play is not just about appearances deceiving. Part of Cyrano's inner gold is his loyal-

Swords and the Swordsman

The sword that Cyrano (and his friends and opponents) would have used is the rapier—a relatively lightweight one-handed weapon used for both stabbing and slashing. In a sense, the rapier was a "transitional" weapon, coming between the heavy broadswords which were used to break through plate armor (or at least break the bone under the armor...in the charming hope that your opponent would develop an infection which would keep him out of combat or, better still, kill him outright!) and the court- or small sword, the very lightweight sword which is the precursor of the modern-day fencer's foil. Where the broadsword demanded two-handed slashing and hacking, and the epee required small, precise, targeted motion, the rapier demanded a combination of the two: the round, sweeping cuts and thrusts of (for example) an old swashbuckler movie.

Unlike a swashbuckler movie, however, rapier fighting wasn't tidy, one-weapon, no tricks fighting. The smart fencer (and Cyrano *was* smart) used his sword—and sometimes a dagger, or a cloak (wrapped around his left arm, to parry with, or flying free, the better to blind your opponent), or a chair or a loaf of bread or a tankard of ale...well, whatever came to hand. While there were rules and styles of fencing, the bottom line was: it was your life on the line, and whatever worked, *worked*.

Swashbuckling, by the way, is a term considerably older than Cyrano would have been. Bucklers were small, round shields (about the size of a modern hub cap) often used with rapiers. If you were one of the local toughs and felt like blowing off some steam, you might walk through the streets of your town, banging on your buckler with the hilt of your sword. This was the equivalent of saying "Okay, who thinks he's man enough to take me on?" and was a challenge that rarely went unmet. Doing this—whacking your buckler with your sword—was called (you guessed it) swashing your buckler, or swashbuckling!

Anatomy of a Rapier

Basket Hilt—Protects hands

Quillons—Good for catching opponent's blade.

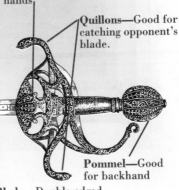

Pommel—Good for backhand

Blade—Double-edged

Roxane, at first, is not loyal. She expects loyalty, but during the course of the play she learns the value of loyalty in loss.

At the end of the last century, after years of plays about the worthlessness of human beings and the meaningless of life, *Cyrano de Bergerac* was a profound success. Rostand celebrates successfully the greatness of the human spirit with his noble characters, their wit and verve, and his brilliant depiction of undying love. A hundred years later, this play is still being produced, and read, and loved, by people who want, just for a little while, to step into the shoes of a man who was larger than life.

say about Cyrano's self-image? If you look at passages when he talks about himself, or makes comments to himself, is he as arrogant as de Guiche and others assume?

•Discuss the sense of honor held by the heroes of this play. Is this kind of honor sufficient justification for ending someone's life? Could one live by that code today—and would one want to? What part does compromise play in this sense of honor?

•What other books or plays contain characters who are ugly on the outside but beautiful inside, and vice versa? How realistic are these characters when compared to real people in modern life? Do these characters, as symbols, have any value for modern life?

Study Questions

•In his death scene, Cyrano reviles against the ancient foes that he has fought: Falsehood, Compromise, Bigotry, Cowardice, and Foolishness. Find examples of each of the "foes" that he confronted during the course of the play.

•In modern terms, what can you

About the Essayist:

Sherwood Smith holds an M.A. from U.C. Santa Barbara; she is the author of numerous adult and young adult fantasy and science fiction books, including *Wren's War* (HBJ '95), and *Rifter's Covenant* (Tor '95). Ms. Smith teaches at Carden Conservatory.